Pop!
Air and Water
Pressure

Stephanie Paris

Consultants

Timothy Rasinski, Ph.D.
Kent State University

Lori Oczkus
Literacy Consultant

Katie McKissick
Physical Science Consultant

Based on writing from
TIME For Kids. *TIME For Kids* and the *TIME For Kids* logo are registered trademarks of TIME Inc. Used under license.

Publishing Credits

Dona Herweck Rice, *Editor-in-Chief*
Lee Aucoin, *Creative Director*
Jamey Acosta, *Senior Editor*
Heidi Fiedler, *Editor*
Lexa Hoang, *Designer*
Stephanie Reid, *Photo Editor*
Emily Engle, *Contributing Author*
Rachelle Cracchiolo, *M.S.Ed., Publisher*

Image Credits: pp.19 (top), 28 (top), 29 (top), 56 Alamy; pp.40, 45, 57 (top) Bigstock; p.6 gbrummett/Flickr; p.47 David Brown; p.16 Getty Images; p.29 (bottom) Verena Tunnicliffe/AFP/Newscom; p.25 (bottom) L. Birmingham/Custom Medical Stock Photo/Newscom; p.19 (bottom) Richard Thomason/KRT/Newscom; p.35 (top) Zuma Press/Newscom; pp.15, 27, 37 (top), 38–39 (illustrations) Kevin Panter; p.31 (illustration) Matthew Tiongco; pp.7, 11, 12–13, 32–33, 43, 52–53 (illustrations) Timothy J. Bradley; pp.17 (top), 21 (top), 23 (top), 28 (bottom), 41, 48, 50–51, 51 (top) Photo Researchers; p.18 Pathathai Chungyam/Getty Images/iStockphoto; All other images from Shutterstock.

Teacher Created Materials

5301 Oceanus Drive
Huntington Beach, CA 92649-1030
http://www.tcmpub.com
ISBN 978-1-4333-4939-3
© 2013 Teacher Created Materials, Inc.

Table of Contents

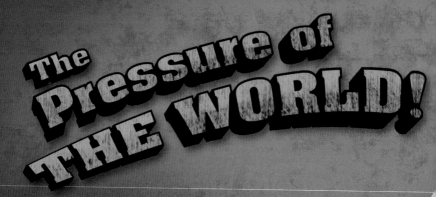

The Pressure of THE WORLD!

Have you ever known someone who had the weight of the world on his or her shoulders? Ancient Greeks believed there was a god named Atlas who actually held up the world by lifting it on his shoulders! But the truth is, we are all under **pressure** every day. In fact, without it, we wouldn't be able to survive!

Atlas

THINK LINK

✦ What is pressure?

✦ Where do we encounter pressure?

✦ What are some ways we can use pressure to our advantage?

5

Pressure

Pressure is a force that pushes against something. There is no escaping pressure. No matter where we go or what we do, we are experiencing it. As you sit reading this book, your fingers press into the page and your body presses into the chair. When you write with a pencil, you press down with the graphite. When you erase, you must apply pressure with the eraser. But even if you were floating in a pool of water doing nothing, you would still be under pressure. The water would be pressing in from all sides, and the air would be pressing down from above. Water and air pressure are two essential forces that affect us every day.

When a water balloon pops, the result is dramatic—and wet.

Pop It! Whop It!

Ever wonder why balloons make that loud popping sound? It has to do with the latex they are made from.

The pressure of the gas inside the balloon puts stress on the latex. The stress causes cracks to form in the latex, and the air rushes out. This happens faster than the speed of sound. It causes small sonic booms!

Next, the latex pieces snap back into their original shape. This also happens faster than the speed of sound and causes more sonic booms!

All these little booms occur over such a small amount of time that we hear them as one event: a loud *POP!*

Heavy Hitters

Blaise Pascal and Sir Isaac Newton were gifted mathematicians and scientists. They lived during the seventeenth century. Pascal is best known for studying fluids and creating **barometers**. He also made machines that performed calculations. Newton is best known for creating calculus, an area of math. Calculus is used to study the laws of the universe. With this math, he developed three basic laws of motion that are still studied and used today.

Newtons and Pascals

Because of their work in math and science, the units of measurement used to describe pressure are named after Newton and Pascal.

The **newton** (**N**) is a unit of force. One newton describes the force needed to accelerate one kilogram of **mass** one meter per second squared. Newtons describe weight.

$$N = kg\ \frac{m}{s^2}$$

The **pascal** (**Pa**) is a unit of pressure. One pascal is one newton of force per square meter.

$$Pa = 1\ \frac{n}{m^2}$$

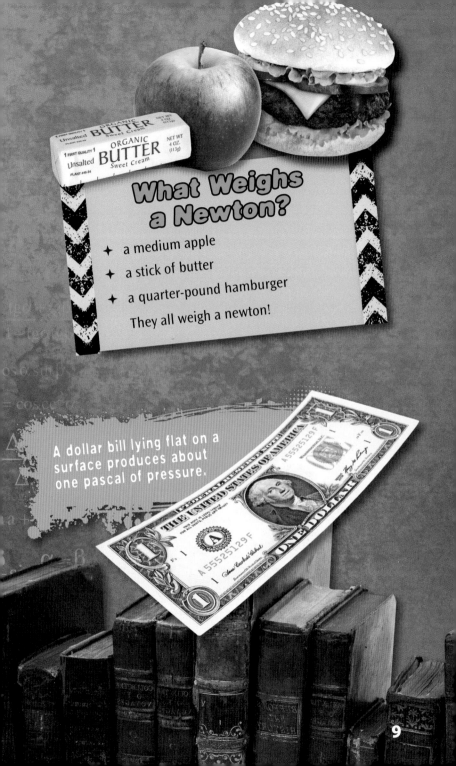

What Weighs a Newton?

✦ a medium apple

✦ a stick of butter

✦ a quarter-pound hamburger

They all weigh a newton!

A dollar bill lying flat on a surface produces about one pascal of pressure.

Water Pressure

When you step into a pool of water, your body feels a change. You can feel the temperature and the pressure of the water on your skin. If you dive down at the deep end of the pool, you feel even more pressure.

When water molecules push on objects around them, they create water pressure. This is because the water has mass. When you turn on a garden hose, the hose changes from flat and floppy to inflated and firm. The water molecules are pushing out on the hose. When you are at the bottom of the pool, you feel the weight of all the water above you pressing on your body. As you dive deeper, you feel more pressure because there is more water above you pressing down.

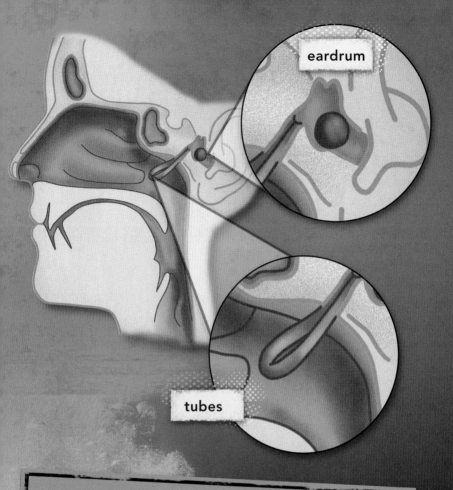

eardrum

tubes

Feeling the Pressure

Have your ears ever hurt when you were underwater? This is because the thin eardrum separates two tubes. One section leads outside the body through the ear, and the other leads inside the body down the throat. Usually, the air pressure in both places is equal. But when diving underwater, there is more pressure from the outside. This can push on the eardrum and even break it!

Holes in a Bottle

In this experiment, you will see water pressure in action!

Materials

- 2-liter soda bottle
- 1 pushpin
- tape
- food coloring
- large cooking tray or sink

Use a pushpin to poke a line of holes in the side of the soda bottle. (Get a grown-up to help you.)

Step 2

Cover all the holes with one long piece of tape. Fill the bottle with water. You can add food coloring if you like. Put the bottle in a large cooking tray or sink (or do this experiment outside). Now, pull off the tape!

Whoa!

The water from the holes at the bottom will spurt out farther than the ones at the top. This is because there is more pressure pushing on the water at the bottom. What happens if you gently squeeze the bottle in different places?

Plants Under Pressure

Plants rely on water pressure for survival. Have you ever seen a plant that has wilted? Everything droops limply as if the plant were feeling depressed. This is because each plant cell contains a **vacuole** for holding water. When the plant is healthy and has a sufficient water supply, the water pushes on the cell from within, making it firm and rigid. It stiffens the plant's leaves and stem. But plants need water for other things, too. They use it for **photosynthesis** and to carry nutrients. These processes are very important to plants. If plants don't have enough water, they take some from the vacuoles. Without the internal water pressure, plants get limp. However, if more water is added, plants can grow perky once more!

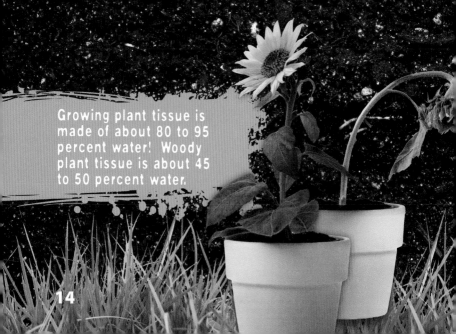

Growing plant tissue is made of about 80 to 95 percent water! Woody plant tissue is about 45 to 50 percent water.

Going Against Gravity

Xylem is the tissue of a plant that carries water from the roots up to the leaves. The plant uses water pressure to make this work. Water evaporates from the leaves. This makes the water pressure at the top of the plant lower than the pressure at the bottom. So water flows up!

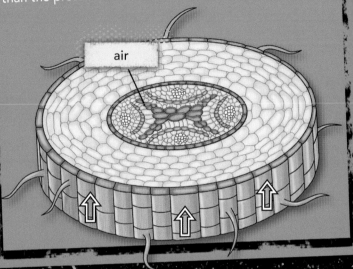

air

Turgor Pressure

Water pressure is so important to plant life that there's a special name for it. Inside cells, it's called **turgor pressure**.

Animals Under Pressure

People and other animals don't have turgor pressure. But we still rely on water pressure for some of our basic needs. Our circulatory system uses pressure to keep us alive. Blood (which is mostly made of water) is pumped through our bodies when the heart squeezes and puts pressure on the fluid.

Blood pressure is a measure of the amount of pressure blood puts on the veins as it moves around the body. It is measured at two points. **Systolic pressure** is measured when the heart beats. **Diastolic pressure** is observed when the heart is resting. Blood pressure needs to stay in a safe range for our bodies to stay healthy. Low blood pressure is rarely a problem over time. But if it develops suddenly, it can be a sign of illness. High blood pressure is thought of as a disease. It can put too much stress on the organs and damage the body over time. About one in three adults in the United States has high blood pressure.

A man gets his blood pressure tested.

Brain Pillow

You probably know your brain is protected by your skull. But did you know it also has a layer of pressurized fluid keeping it safe? A watery fluid prevents your brain from hitting the inside of your skull every time you move. If the pressure of this fluid is too low, the brain is unprotected. If it gets too high, it can actually end up squishing the brain instead of cushioning it.

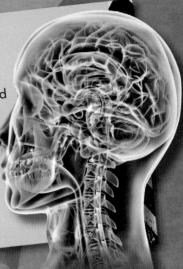

On a blood-pressure monitor, the top number shows systolic pressure and the bottom number shows diastolic pressure.

Blood Pressure Chart

Category	Systolic		Diastolic
Low	less than 90	or	less than 60
Normal	between 90–120	or	between 60–80
Should Be Watched	120–139	or	80–89
High, Stage 1	140–159	or	90–99
High, Stage 2	160 or over	or	100 or over

17

Bodies in Water

If you dive into a pool, what forces act on your body? **Buoyancy**, also called **upthrust**, is the force that pushes up an object in a fluid. The object seems to lose weight. This happens because molecules lower in the fluid are more densely packed than molecules above. Objects are forced up, away from the area of greater pressure and into the area of less pressure.

A Sweet Surprise

Scientists wanted to know if it's possible to swim in syrup. They found 16 volunteers. Then, they timed them when they swam in a pool of regular water. Next, they mixed in 660 pounds of guar gum, which is used to thicken things like shampoo and ice cream. This made a pool that was filled with gooey, syrupy glop. It was twice as thick as water. One scientist said it reminded him of snot! Participants all swam with times very close to their original water times. And neither water nor glop seemed to give any consistent advantage.

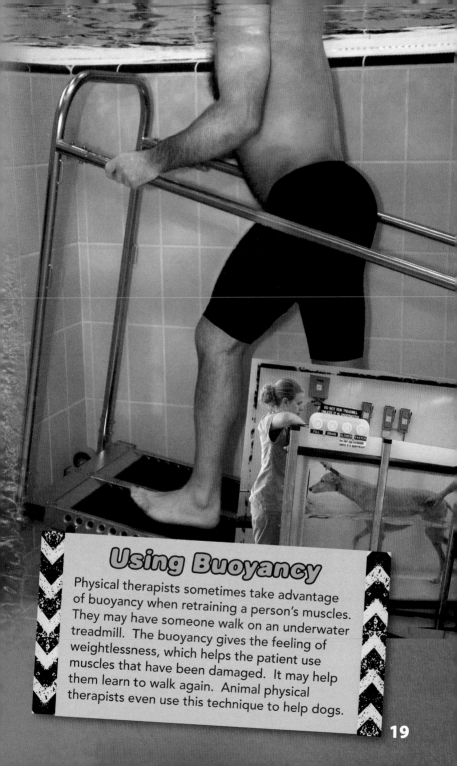

Using Buoyancy

Physical therapists sometimes take advantage of buoyancy when retraining a person's muscles. They may have someone walk on an underwater treadmill. The buoyancy gives the feeling of weightlessness, which helps the patient use muscles that have been damaged. It may help them learn to walk again. Animal physical therapists even use this technique to help dogs.

19

Water Density

The salt level and temperature of the ocean determines its **density**. The saltier the water is, the denser it is. And the cooler the water is, the denser it is. So the water closest to the surface is generally warmer and less salty than the water deeper below. But there is a catch. Heat changes things more than salt. So warmer, saltier layers of water can rest on top of cooler, less salty ones. The result is that oceans are made up of layers of water based on their density.

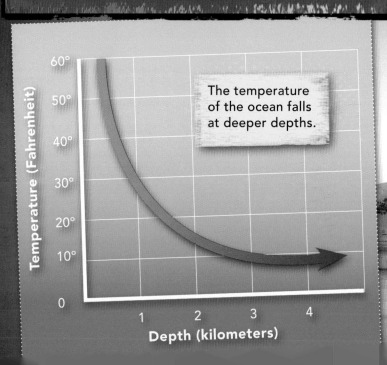

The temperature of the ocean falls at deeper depths.

Try This

Take two containers and fill each with tap water. Add six tablespoons of salt to one container. Stir until the salt dissolves. (It's okay if there are a few crystals still at the bottom.) Now, place a raw egg in each container. Which one floats? The one in the salt water will float because the water is now denser than the egg!

Floating

Why do some objects float in water while others sink? Consider this: If you toss a metal paper clip into a swimming pool, it will sink. But huge ships can carry millions of tons of cargo across the ocean. How can this be?

If the force of upthrust, or buoyancy, on an object is greater than the force of **gravity**, it will float. That means if an object displaces more water than its weight, it floats. The paper clip does not displace a large amount of water, so it sinks. But enormous vessels are built to take advantage of upthrust. Their shape allows them to displace enough water so they can float.

Archimedes' Principle

Archimedes was the ancient Greek scientist who figured out that if something displaces more water than its weight, it will float. So now this concept is named after him. It is called **Archimedes' Principle.**

Try This

Fill a container with water and grab a variety of objects. (Hint: Don't choose anything that might be damaged if it gets wet!) Look for balls, pen caps, bottle caps, crayons, paper boats, or rubber bands. First, guess which things will sink and which ones will float. Then, try them out! Were you right?

Tipping the Scales

Here's another way to look at it. First, a metal block is weighed in air. Then, it is weighed in water. The upward buoyant force of the water causes the scale to measure the block as a lighter weight.

air measurement

water measurement

Pressure of the Deep

The deeper you get in the ocean, the more pressure is put on your body. How much pressure? The lowest known point on Earth is thought to be in the Mariana Trench in the Pacific Ocean. At this deepest part of the ocean, there are 16,000 pounds of pressure on every square inch of matter!

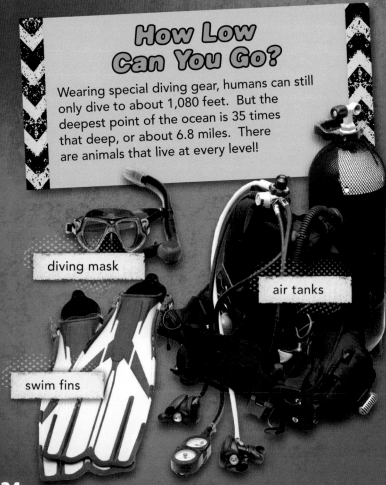

How Low Can You Go?

Wearing special diving gear, humans can still only dive to about 1,080 feet. But the deepest point of the ocean is 35 times that deep, or about 6.8 miles. There are animals that live at every level!

diving mask

air tanks

swim fins

gas bubbles
form in blood
vessels and
tissues

bubbles
blocking
blood
vessels

The Bends

Decompression sickness, sometimes called *the bends*, happens when divers breathe gas (air) at high pressures when they are deep underwater. As divers come up to the surface, the gas that is dissolved in the blood comes out and forms bubbles. It can be very painful and even deadly. The trick is to come up slowly. This lets the body adjust to the new levels of pressure and reabsorb any gas bubbles before they get large enough to do damage.

25

Deep Sea Challenge

The Mariana Trench is a 1,500-mile-long scar in the sea floor of the Pacific Ocean. Its deepest spot is named Challenger Deep. Fifty years ago, researchers made the trip down. But they could only stay at the bottom for 20 minutes. **Silt** kept them from taking any photos.

On March 26, 2012, a special submarine called the *Deepsea Challenger* went to the ocean floor again. The person inside the craft was actually not a scientist. It was film director James Cameron! After filming the movie *Titanic*, he grew passionate about exploring the deep sea. So he decided to make it his own project. The **data** from his trip is still being looked at, but he reports that even at this extreme depth there was life. He was able to see tiny fish and shrimp-like creatures from inside his vessel.

How Low Can You Go?

One pascal is one newton of force per square meter. Another measurement of force is *psi*. It is the number of pounds of pressure on every square inch of an object.

What	Pounds Per Square Inch (psi)
a dollar bill resting on a surface	.0001 psi
pressure of 1 pint of water in a 1" x 1" tube	1 psi
ocean pressure on a submarine at a depth of 6,500 meters (m)	10,000 psi

How Low Did It Go?

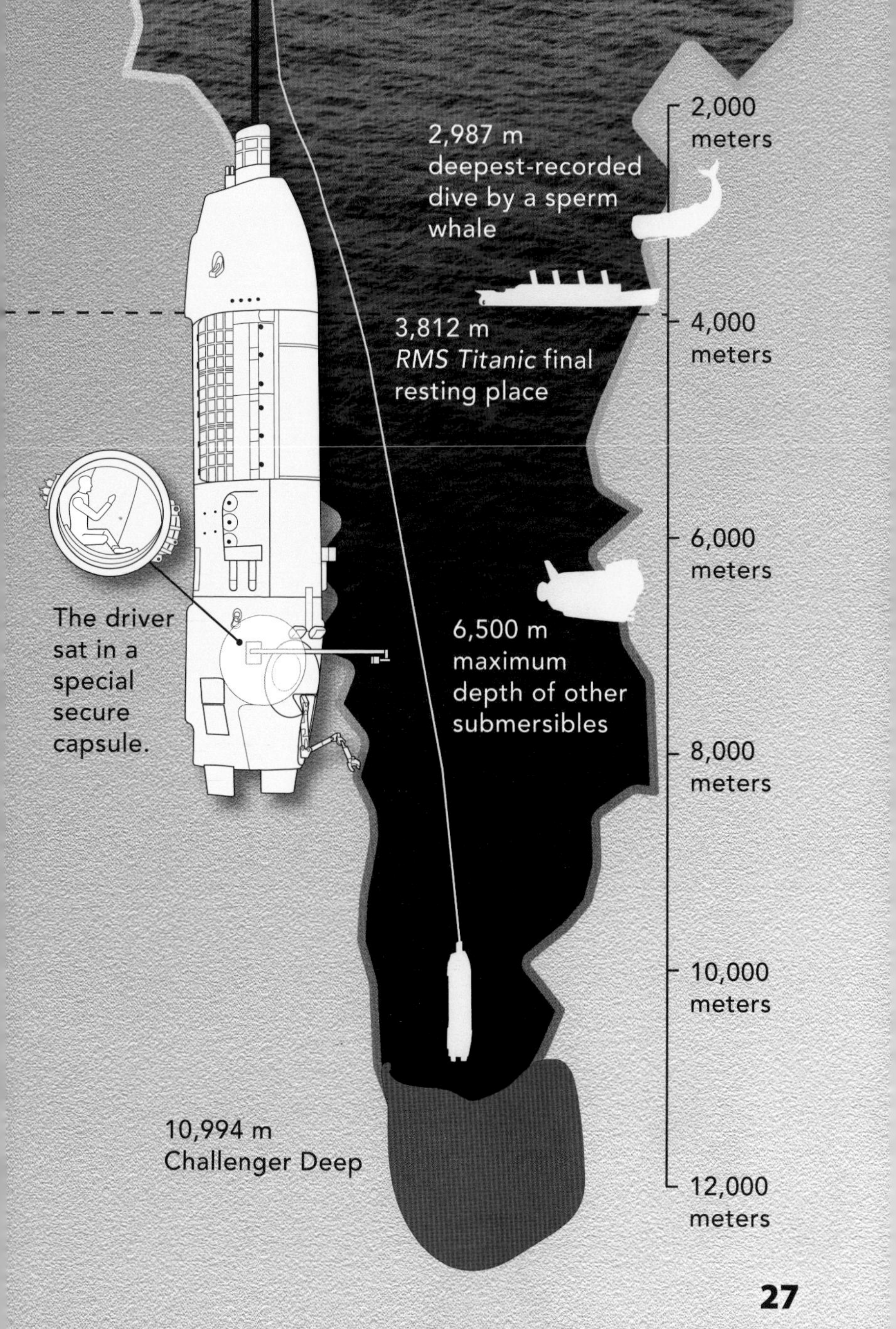

2,987 m
deepest-recorded
dive by a sperm
whale

3,812 m
RMS Titanic final
resting place

The driver
sat in a
special
secure
capsule.

6,500 m
maximum
depth of other
submersibles

10,994 m
Challenger Deep

— 2,000
meters

— 4,000
meters

— 6,000
meters

— 8,000
meters

— 10,000
meters

— 12,000
meters

27

Creatures of the Abyss

These creatures have evolved and adapted over time to live on the ocean floor at extreme depths. Read about where they live and how they survive there.

Viperfish

Found about one mile down, these creepy critters have a serious overbite! Some are colored black as night. But others have no coloring at all. Many have organs on their bodies that light up to lure prey into their waiting jaws.

Fangtooth

These small fish look ferocious but only grow to about six inches long. Their large mouths allow them to catch prey whole, and their stomachs stretch to let them swallow creatures whole!

Giant Squid

These mysterious creatures live deep in the ocean and can grow up to 60 feet in length. They may live as deep as 10,000 feet below the surface. But scientists know very little else about them. This is because they have never been observed alive in the wild. Dead squid have been found floating or washed up on the shore. And they have been found inside the stomachs of sperm whales, which like to eat them.

Giant Tube Worm

Up to eight feet long with brightly colored red fringe, these guys stand out in a crowd! What is even more impressive, though, is the way they eat. Giant tube worms live near vents of hot water. Inside the worms, bacteria change chemicals from the vents into food for the worms.

Water Pressure in Action

How often do you use a garden hose, a spray bottle, a water gun, a toilet, a sink, or a shower? You interact with water pressure every day. When you turn on a faucet or flush a toilet, water pressure helps you in a very basic way. You can get a drink, clean yourself, or dispose of waste by using the pressure of water.

If the pressure level is wrong, you can have a problem. If the pressure in your shower is too low, water will just trickle out. If it is too high, it can be painful and make a mess. Using and controlling water pressure is a daily part of our lives.

Water Rides

Many amusement park rides use water pressure to create fun thrills. Water pressure pumps water to the top of tall waterslides.

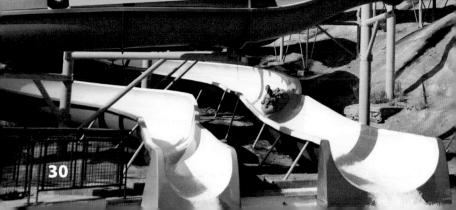

Water Jets

Personal watercraft use a jet engine to make a strong stream of water. The engine is attached to an impeller. The impeller is like a rotor on an airplane with curved blades that spin. It pulls water from below the craft and forces it through a nozzle located behind the machine. This squirts water out forcefully behind the machine. Since every action has an equal and opposite reaction, the backward force causes the watercraft to move forward!

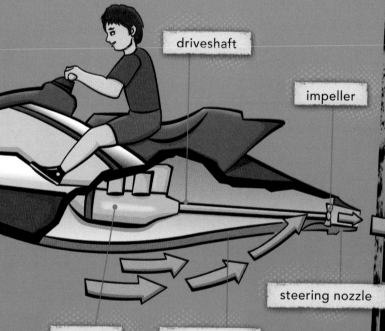

driveshaft

impeller

steering nozzle

engine

intake grate

The Inside Story

Spray bottles are a great example of an everyday object that relies on water pressure. Cleaning supplies, hairspray, insect repellent, and perfume are just some of the liquids that come in spray bottles. Have you ever stopped to think about how the liquid gets from the inside of the bottle out through the nozzle? The answer is water pressure!

Step 1

When you pull the trigger, you add energy to the system. The squeeze forces a small ball to move in the tube.

Step 2

New liquid rushes in to fill the empty space in the tube. Usually, the first pump doesn't spray anything because there isn't liquid in the tube yet.

STOP! THINK...

- How do these diagrams change the way you understand how a spray bottle works?

- Have you ever tried to use a spray bottle that wouldn't work? What might be going wrong with the spray bottle?

- Why do you think spray bottles aren't used for thicker liquids such as honey or syrup?

Step 3

When the small ball moves in the tube, it increases pressure inside the pump and forces any liquid inside the tube out the nozzle.

Step 4

The nozzle also has a small ball inside. When you release the trigger, the ball closes the nozzle again, keeping air from entering from the outside and maintaining pressure within the pump.

Changing Pressure

Many things can affect water pressure. One simple way to change pressure is to force water through smaller or larger openings. Have you ever put your thumb over the nozzle of a hose to make the water spray farther and faster? The same amount of water is trying to get through a smaller space, so it must accelerate to get through. It has more pressure, so it spurts farther. What do you think would happen if you created a larger hole for the water to pass through?

GPM

Gallons per minute is also called *gpm* for short. It is the rate at which a liquid flows out of something, such as a hose. Faucets flow around 2.5 gpm, but you can find more efficient faucets that have lower gpm rates. A typical garden hose allows water to flow at about 5 to 10 gpm. While this rate varies, a fire hose can flow around 95 to 200 gpm, and some firefighting trucks can pump as much as 1,500 gpm! That's a lot of water!

A High-Pressure Job!

A firefighter **engineer** must know a great deal about water pressure. At a fire, the engineer is in charge of the equipment that affects the water pressure directed to the fire hoses. A pump in the fire engine creates water pressure. The engineer decides which valves to open. The valves adjust the water pressure and direct the water into certain hoses. Another group of firefighters controls the nozzle. The engineer must decide on the right level of water pressure to put the fire out quickly and safely.

Hydraulics

Hydraulics is the study of how to use liquids in machines. In simple terms, it is water power. Early Greeks used hydraulics to **irrigate** their farms. They even made water-based clocks. Today, hydraulic machines are used in construction.

How Hydraulics Work

A simple hydraulic system has two pistons joined by a fluid-filled pipe. Often, oil is the fluid used because it can stand up to the heat. An engine provides force that presses down one piston, causing the other piston to go up. The force can be increased by changing the sizes of the two pistons and their chambers.

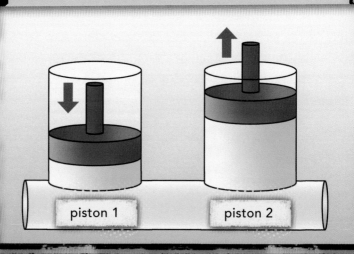

piston 1

piston 2

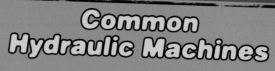

Common Hydraulic Machines

- ✦ auto brakes
- ✦ elevators
- ✦ bulldozers
- ✦ forklifts
- ✦ backhoes
- ✦ cranes
- ✦ shovels
- ✦ loaders
- ✦ Jaws of Life

Water Wheels

Some of the earliest hydraulic machines were waterwheels. These machines used the force of a river or stream to rotate a large wooden wheel. The wheel had an axle that could be used to turn a series of gears. Early waterwheels were used to turn heavy stones that milled grains into flour.

Dams and Turbines

Dams are built to block a river or other body of water. Sometimes, they are simply used to control water. But if they are combined with **turbines** that make electricity, they can be a powerful tool for creating energy. Waterpower creates 19 to 24 percent of the world's electricity. And it provides one billion people with power.

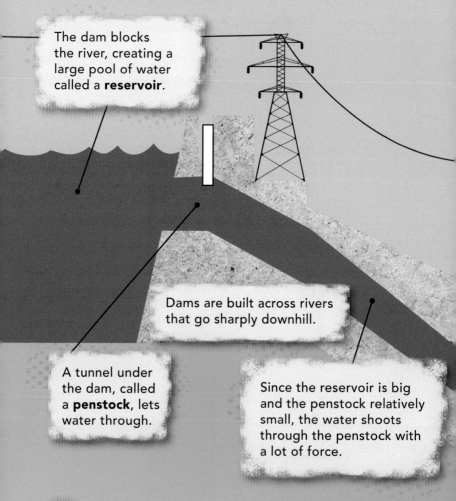

The dam blocks the river, creating a large pool of water called a **reservoir**.

Dams are built across rivers that go sharply downhill.

A tunnel under the dam, called a **penstock**, lets water through.

Since the reservoir is big and the penstock relatively small, the water shoots through the penstock with a lot of force.

Drawbacks to Dams

Dams are clean and efficient. But they are not without problems. Creating a dam floods a large area of land. And the dam can cause problems for wildlife. Sockeye salmon and trout numbers in the northwestern United States have dropped from 16 million to 2.5 million since hydroelectric dams were built on the Columbia River.

The turbines are attached to a generator.

As the water turns the turbine, metal magnets spin around metal coils, producing electricity.

A turbine or a series of turbines lie inside the dam.

Air Pressure

We don't usually think of air and water as having similar qualities. But they have more in common than you might think. Gases and liquids are both fluids, which means they behave in similar ways. They both flow. Like water, air has mass and weight, and therefore, it generates pressure. And this pressure can be used in many helpful ways.

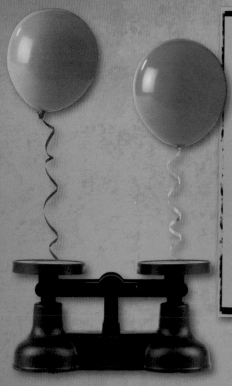

Balancing Act

Try blowing up two balloons with the same amount of air and place them on opposite sides of a balance. Make sure the two sides are equal. Take one balloon off the balance and pinch the rubber near the bottom where the tie is. Using a pin or scissors, make a small hole in the pinched rubber. Then, slowly let the air out of the balloon. Put the empty balloon back on the balance. Does it weigh more or less than the balloon with the air still in it?

Achoo!

When you sneeze, your body violently forces air out. In fact, the average sneeze travels around 40 miles per hour!

Bodies in Balance

If the air surrounding us has weight, why doesn't it squash us? The reason is that we have air inside us, too! There are pockets of air in our lungs, between our cells, and inside our ears. And much of the rest of us is made of water. Between the water and air pressing on our bodies from the inside and the air pressing on us from the outside, our bodies are in balance.

air → water ← air
air

Breathe In Breathe Out

Air pressure is essential to our survival. Without air pressure, we couldn't breathe. We couldn't circulate oxygen through our bodies. But perhaps more importantly, air pressure protects Earth by creating an atmosphere. This protective bubble allows all life on the planet to thrive.

How to Drink Through a Straw

1. Lower the air pressure in your mouth (in other words, suck air in).
2. Wait while the outside air tries to equalize the pressure. Oh no! There is liquid in the way!
3. The air pushes down on the liquid, forcing it up the straw.
4. Enjoy your delicious beverage!

Lungs

How do we inhale? Our lungs expand and create a lower-pressure zone inside them. Air rushes in to equalize the pressure. Exhaling works the opposite way. Our lungs **contract**, increasing pressure and forcing the air into the lower-pressure zone of the atmosphere!

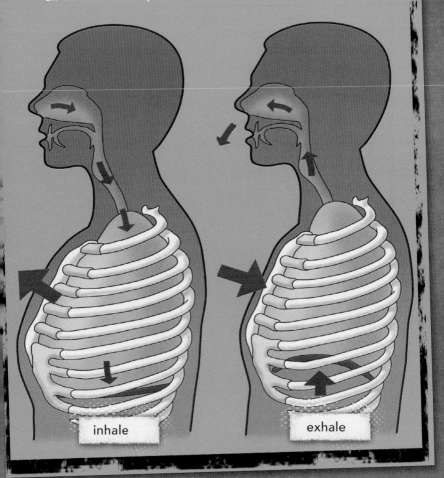

inhale

exhale

Atmosphere

Earth is surrounded by a mixture of gases we call *air*. There are thousands of tons of air molecules in the atmosphere. The molecules are all held there by Earth's gravity. The closer to Earth you are, the more densely packed the air molecules are. At sea level, the pressure is measured in atmospheres. One atmosphere is equal to about 14.7 pounds per square inch of pressure. If you go above sea level, the pressure is lower, and if you go below sea level, the pressure is greater.

Mountain Climbing

While deep sea divers deal with greater pressure on their bodies, mountain climbers must adjust to less pressure. At a high **altitude**, oxygen molecules are fewer and farther between. Going slowly can help climbers' bodies adjust to changes in pressure and oxygen levels. At some altitudes, climbers must use oxygen tanks.

Cooking at High Altitudes

Have you ever seen a recipe that included high-altitude directions? Cooking times and temperatures vary depending on whether food is made at sea level or above. This is because of the change in pressure. Boiling happens when water breaks its molecular bonds, changing from a liquid state into steam. At sea level, water boils at 212° F (100° C). But when there is less pressure on the water, it takes less energy to break the bonds and water is able to boil at a lower temperature! That means it can take less time to cook a dish at higher altitudes.

Earth's atmosphere is about 60 miles thick.

The Vacuum of Space

High above Earth's atmosphere in outer space, there isn't any air, so there isn't any air pressure. Instead, there is a **vacuum**. A perfect vacuum has no matter in it at all. But no vacuum is truly perfect. Outer space has very, very little matter in it. There are only a few hydrogen atoms per cubic meter.

" Nature abhors a vacuum. "
—Traditional Greek saying that means where a vacuum exists, matter tends to fill it

Vacuum Cleaner

If a vacuum has nothing in it, why is a vacuum cleaner called a vacuum? They are usually filled with dirt! A perfect vacuum has nothing in it. But another way to think about vacuums is in terms of air pressure. Vacuums create negative air pressure. Vacuum cleaners are a kind of **low vacuum**. They suck particles in because they create an area of pressure that is lower than the pressure of the air around them. In other words, vacuum cleaners aren't so much sucking in the dirt as the air pressure around them pushes things into the lower-pressure zone.

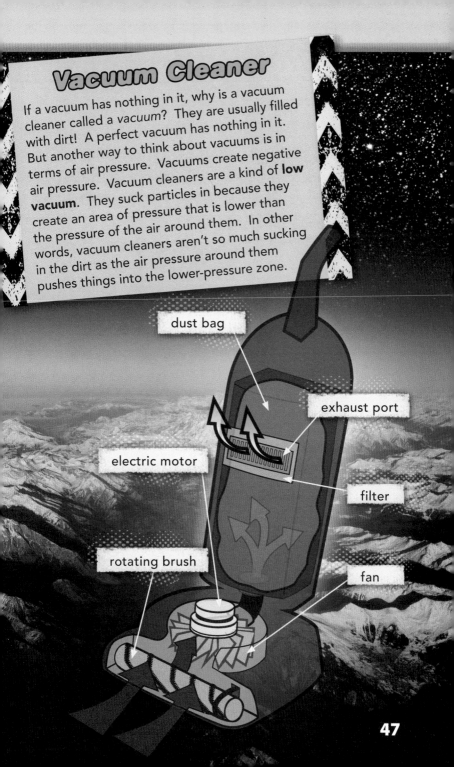

dust bag

exhaust port

electric motor

filter

rotating brush

fan

Heating Up

When a fluid such as air or water is exposed to a heat source, the molecules begin to travel. They bounce around and spread out in various directions. Molecules that are more spread out are less dense. So, generally speaking, warmer fluids are at lower pressures.

But what if you heat something up and keep it in a confined space so it can't expand? In that case, the molecules start to push out on the container. Pressure inside the system can build quickly!

Convection

Convection is the circular movement in a fluid caused by heat. Warmer, less dense fluids tend to rise, and cooler, denser fluids sink.

Hot-Air Balloon

Hot-air balloons work by taking advantage of the lower density of the heated air. A burner heats the air that fills a balloon made of very light weight fabric. A basket hangs below. The balloonist is inside. The warm air has a lower density than the cooler air near the Earth. As the warm air gets pushed up, it takes the balloon and the balloonist with it. By adjusting the amount of warm air inside the balloon, the balloonist can adjust the altitude.

Weather

Why are some days cloudy while other days are windy? Where do tornadoes come from? And how do weather forecasters predict what type of weather will happen next? Weather is extremely complicated. But much of what we know about weather can be explained through an understanding of air and water pressure. Over 70 percent of Earth is covered in water. And the entire planet is surrounded by air. The sun provides heat. The interaction of these three elements creates weather.

Weather

Wind is created when air flows from high-pressure areas to low-pressure areas. Cooler, dense air sinks, and warmer, less dense air rises. But that's not the whole story. Because Earth is rotating, the air doesn't just sink and rise—it also shifts. Nearer to the ground, friction from Earth slows the air down.

The Earth's rotation causes three main wind currents. Blue arrows represent cold air currents. Red arrows represent warm air currents.

Night and Day

Wind is usually much stronger during the day. This is because the sun is actively heating the air. This causes convection currents.

Atmospheric Pressure

Atmospheric pressure does not stay the same all the time. Warmth, moisture, and other factors change the pressure of the surrounding air. If the pressure readings are low, this can reveal that a storm is on the way. This is because air likes to move from high to low pressure. So if you are in a low-pressure zone, you are where the air is going to be moving to! The weather changes as the pressure changes. Luckily, the pressure can easily be measured using a barometer.

Materials:

Build Your Own Barometer

- 1 large glass jar or coffee can
- plastic wrap or a balloon
- 1 straw
- 1 rubber band
- lined paper
- tape
- scissors

Step 1

If you are using a balloon, cut off the bottom half and stretch it over your container. If you are using plastic wrap, stretch it tightly over your container. Either way, you want a tight, smooth seal. Use the rubber band to secure the cover. You want to make sure no air can get in or out.

Step 2

Lay the straw on top of the plastic. Let about two-thirds of the straw hang over the edge. Tape the straw in place.

Step 3

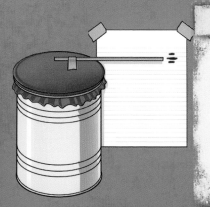

Place your new barometer in front of a piece of lined paper against the wall. Record where the straw points on the paper. When the pressure changes, the straw will move up and down. Record your results as the weather changes over the next few months.

Thunderstorms

Thunderstorms usually form on hot, humid summer days. Warm convection currents cause tall thunderclouds. These are called **cumulonimbus** clouds. The warm air rises up into the cooler layers of the atmosphere. Then, inside the cloud, water and ice particles rise up and drop back down over and over. They are following the pressure cycle of the air. Eventually, ice crystals in the cloud become so heavy that they fall to Earth as rain or hail. At the same time, high winds in the cloud cause friction. The friction charges up particles until lightning strikes. Then, the energy is released.

Hurricanes

A small thunderstorm forms over warm water. The water warms the air above it, causing a rising current of heated air. Cooler air gets pulled in to replace the rising warm air. Soon, huge banks of cumulonimbus clouds have formed around a circular column of warm air in the middle. This is now a hurricane. And the column of air in the middle is the eye of the storm!

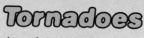

Tornadoes

Tornadoes form when winds inside thunderclouds begin to spin out of control. A funnel of warm air forms and drops down to the ground. Once it is formed, a tornado can move across the ground at 60 miles per hour!

The Power of Pressure

People have been intrigued by the power of water and air since time began. Water and air are around us all the time. If we are deprived of either one for very long, we will die. Water and air pressure can do some powerful things. Wind can push ships out to sea, carry seeds from afar, or knock down homes in an instant. Water falls from the sky as rain, takes things from place to place, and can wash entire cities away in a flood. But water and air pressure are also involved in small but vital things such as taking a breath or watering a garden. No matter what you do, you are sure to experience the power of pressure today!

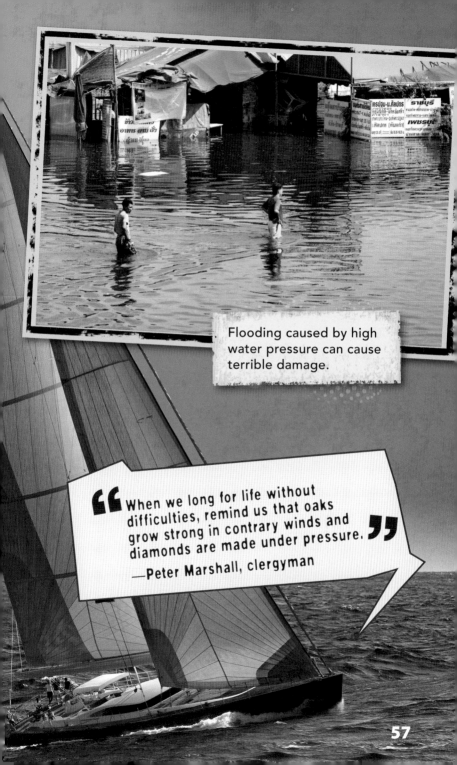

Flooding caused by high water pressure can cause terrible damage.

> When we long for life without difficulties, remind us that oaks grow strong in contrary winds and diamonds are made under pressure.
> —Peter Marshall, clergyman

Glossary

altitude—the vertical distance of an object above a given level (such as sea level)

Archimedes' Principle—the idea that things which displace more water than their weight will float

atmospheric pressure—the force of the air pushing against a surface

barometers—devices used to measure air pressure and predict weather patterns

buoyancy—the force pushing objects up in liquid

contract—to draw or squeeze together to become smaller

convection—the circular movement in a fluid caused by heat

cumulonimbus—a dense, puffy cloud with a low base and a wide top; often an indicator of a thunderstorm

data—facts and statistics collected together for analysis

density—the quality of having a high mass per unit of volume

diastolic pressure—the blood pressure when the heart is at rest

engineer—a person who runs or manages an engine or technical machinery

gravity— the pull of any object with mass

irrigate—to supply water to land or crops to help them grow

low vacuum—the amount of vacuum that can be achieved with relatively simple equipment

mass—the amount of matter something is made of

newton (N)—a unit of force needed to accelerate one kilogram of mass one meter per second squared

pascal (Pa)—a unit of pressure; one newton of force per square meter

penstock—a tunnel under a dam designed to let water through

photosynthesis—the process by which a green plant turns water and carbon dioxide into food when the plant is exposed to light

pressure—the application of force to something by something else in direct contact with it

reservoir—the water that builds up behind a dam

silt—a mixture of very small rocks and particles of soil in water

systolic pressure—the blood pressure when the heart beats

turbine—a machine used for producing continuous power

turgor pressure—the water pressure inside plant cells

upthrust—another word for *buoyancy*

vacuole—the part of a plant cell that holds water

vacuum—a space completely empty of matter

xylem—the tissue of a plant that carries water from the roots to the leaves

Index

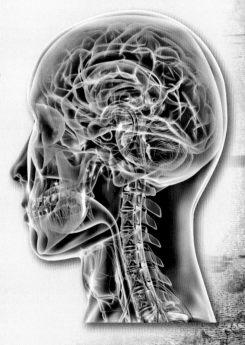

Bibliography

Ellyard, David. *Weather (Nature Company Discoveries Library).* **Time Life Education, 1996.**

You know how weather affects the land, but what is weather exactly? Gain a deeper understanding of what weather is and how it affects the world around us.

Kain, Kathleen E. *Secret Tricks: The Science Spiders Investigate Air Pressure.* **Ranch Works, 1999.**

Dig deeper into the science of air pressure with the help of these friendly spiders. Each story in this book includes a safe, fun experiment you can do at home.

Meiani, Antonella. *Water (Experimenting with Science).* **Lerner Publishing Group, 2002.**

Dozens of experiments help you understand water pressure and the science behind it. With the help of this book, tough scientific theories are made into easily understood ideas.

Spilsbury, Richard. *Air and Water Pressure (Fantastic Forces).* **Heinemann-Raintree, 2007.**

Gain a deeper understanding of how this force works and the role it plays in our lives. Try some exciting hands-on experiments to become a master of air and water pressure!

More to Explore

Deep Sea Challenge
http://deepseachallenge.com/the-expedition/

Learn about James Cameron's exciting expedition to the deepest part of the ocean. Discover the equipment used and the research collected during this dive.

It's a Breeze: How Air Pressure Affects You
http://kids.earth.nasa.gov/archive/air_pressure/index.html

This NASA site for kids has lots of information about air pressure, experiments, games, activities, and discussion questions that will help you really understand the concept.

How Stuff Works: Atmospheric Pressure
http://videos.howstuffworks.com/

Type in *Atmospheric Pressure* in the search bar. Here, you'll watch a video with an experiment demonstrating atmospheric pressure along with an explanation of how and why Earth is designed perfectly for life.

Tree House Weather Kids
http://urbanext.illinois.edu/treehouse/activity_pressure.cfm

Click on *Air Pressure and Wind* at the top. Predicting the weather doesn't happen by accident—it is a science. Get to know the basics about air pressure and wind here, with some help from your new friends.

About the Author

Stephanie Paris is a seventh-generation Californian. She has her Bachelor of Arts in psychology from the University of California, Santa Cruz, and her multiple subject teaching credential from California State University, San Jose. She has been an elementary classroom teacher, an elementary school computer and technology teacher, a home schooling mother, an educational activist, an educational author, a web designer, a blogger, and a Girl Scout leader. Ms. Paris lives in Germany where she is very grateful to be a beneficiary of the mild weather brought on by the Gulf Stream.